DEDICATION

This book is dedicated to my best friend Pat. You have been there for through thick and thin. I think God really wants me happy because He gave me you as my best friend.

TABLE OF CONTENTS

Keep Calm and Plan

How to Conquer Panic and Avoid Its Negative Effects

By: Steven Carter

9781635012972

PUBLISHERS NOTES

Disclaimer – Speedy Publishing LLC

This publication is intended to provide helpful and informative material. It is not intended to diagnose, treat, cure, or prevent any health problem or condition, nor is intended to replace the advice of a physician. No action should be taken solely on the contents of this book. Always consult your physician or qualified health-care professional on any matters regarding your health and before adopting any suggestions in this book or drawing inferences from it.

The author and publisher specifically disclaim all responsibility for any liability, loss or risk, personal or otherwise, which is incurred as a consequence, directly or indirectly, from the use or application of any contents of this book.

Any and all product names referenced within this book are the trademarks of their respective owners. None of these owners have sponsored, authorized, endorsed, or approved this book.

Always read all information provided by the manufacturers' product labels before using their products. The author and publisher are not responsible for claims made by manufacturers.

This book was originally printed before 2014. This is an adapted reprint by Speedy Publishing LLC with newly updated content designed to help readers with much more accurate and timely information and data.

Speedy Publishing LLC

40 E Main Street, Newark, Delaware, 19711

Contact Us: 1-888-248-4521

Website: http://www.speedypublishing.co

REPRINTED Paperback Edition: 9781635012972:

Manufactured in the United States of America

CHAPTER 1- UNDERSTANDING ANXIETY

Your heart is pounding fast and you are feeling dizzy. It seems as though you have to sit down in order for you not to fall. You are having trouble catching your breath. You are experiencing a numbing feeling in your hands and feet.

There is a tightening pressure in your chest area. You think you may be on the verge of a heart attack. You think something is really wrong with you; however, you are far from dying.

Anxiety is a mental disorder in which a person fears just about anything and they think every outcome will turn out for the worst. This fear is frightening because it is so intense and they always fear that someone is after them.

If you have any type of disorder that is associated with anxiety, then your mind will always be focused on being scared for no reason. You will always feel that there is no solution to your unfounded fear and that there is no way out.

You feel paralyzed as though you can't do anything. Basically, you are frozen with fear. This disorder can attack at any time.

Anxiety disorder is more than just one action. Anxiety disorder has different sub-disorders that can fit under this. For instance, there are panic attacks, obsessive compulsive disorder and others that are related to the anxiety disorder family.

There are many people all over that suffer from anxiety attacks. If you are not afflicted with them, you may know someone who is. If it is you, you need to know how to help yourself. If it's someone else, you need to know how to help them. You will have to be understanding and help them to get the treatment and support that they need to combat this condition.

What Causes Anxiety?

There is no one thing that causes this disorder and those that are related to it. You may think that there are certain things that trigger it. Well, there could be and then again, it may be something that just happens. It all depends on how it is perceived.

Those that the anxiety attacks or related disorders may have one attack. Then they may go back to the scene where the initial one took place and have another one. They are reminded of what happened before. They will feel bad and end up having another one without thinking about it. It seems like a constant cycle of intense fear. Then they feel that they will have more attacks.

Believe it or not, it's all in the mind. If you constantly fear and expect to have an anxiety attack or something related to it, then it will happen. The thing about this is people that experience these attacks resent having to hear that it's all in the mind. They feel that people are brushing this off as something that you can get over.

The feeling of anxiety comes from your brain. According to studies that deal with this, there are at least two areas of your brain that help to trigger the sense of fear and anxiety in your mind. It causes your brain to have a defense mechanism and then you react.

However, there can be situations that you may think cause anxiety and related attacks. Some people have so much stress nowadays. It can come from office politics, overwhelming debt, family issues and other events that can bring this on.

There are also some drugs that can trigger an anxiety attack from side effects or withdrawals. This would include alcohol, caffeine, cold medicine, decongestants, nicotine, diet pills and numerous other medications that people take for various ailments and illnesses.

Not eating right can also be a contributor to anxiety. There are some situations, where you may have to take a test or face a lot of people. If you're not ready, you can get nervous or jittery.

Do You Suffer from Anxiety?

There is no certain group on this earth that is a target for anxiety and related attacks or disorders. So, with that said, who do you think suffers from this? Well, it could be anyone. It could be in your family, your friends, co-workers or anyone that you may know.

A lot of times, it could be those that you know and you would have never thought in a million years that they would suffer from something like this.

Unfortunately, these attacks are usually kept secret and not disclosed. This is one of those "sweep under the rug" embarrassment moments. This is not something that is talked about out in the open. Some people will acknowledge dealing with this when they are caught in the act and can't fake it.

Believe it or not, there are people such as politicians and even Hollywood celebrities who suffer from anxiety attacks and related conditions. However, they pay their publicists and others to keep it out of the public eye.

They don't want to be in the spotlight because they have to work on keeping up their image. However, what they may not realize is that someone may be able to benefit from their disclosure.

Unfortunately, for people that have to deal with this, anxiety attacks affect and tend to interfere with those who are trying to live a normal life. If you have excessive anxiety attacks, it can be related to a psychiatric condition. When these attacks become serious and they last a long time, they are considered to be out of the norm.

With the symptoms of an anxiety attack, the brain relays messages to other parts of a person's body. Certain parts of the body, such as the lungs and heart work overtime while the anxiety attack is happening. The brain ends up releasing a lot of adrenaline.

Forms of Anxiety-Rooted Disorders

- **Generalized Anxiety Disorder (GAD)**

Generalized anxiety disorder, or GAD, refers to people that are constant worriers and are always tense. The thing about this is that there really isn't a cause for this, nor is anyone or anything at fault to provoke it. They look for the worst and are always extremely worried about work, family health and money. They even feel anxiety in the course of their normal day.

Steven Carter

If this pattern is consistent for at least six months, a person can be considered as suffering from GAD. They feel that they cannot stop worrying even though the concern is not as great as they make it out to be.

It's difficult for them to relax, they are easily startled by people or noises and they have a hard time focusing. Sometimes they cannot sleep at night or wake up in the morning on their own. Here are some other symptoms that contribute to generalized anxiety disorder:

- Feeling tired
- Aching muscles
- Irritable
- Nauseated
- Sweaty
- Lightheaded
- Shortness of breath
- Frequent trips to the bathroom
- Shaking or trembling
- Hot flashes

If they don't have a high anxiety level and still suffer from generalized anxiety disorder, they can still be employed and be able to interact socially with others. However, if they have GAD on a higher scale, they may have trouble doing and completing simple tasks that others would take for granted.

Close to seven million American adults suffer from generalized anxiety disorders. There are more women (about twice as many) than men that are dealing with this. Even with that, the risk reaches its peak starting at childhood and going through the middle age years. Studies have shown that there are some genes that contribute to people getting GAD.

There are other anxiety disorders that happen in conjunction with GAD, such as substance abuse and depression. If treated properly, the person affected can overcome their worries with whatever problems they are dealing with.

- **Social Anxiety Disorder**

Social anxiety disorder, which is also known as social phobia, happens when a person is extremely self-conscious and anxious. It happens every day in different social situations. They are extremely fearful of being watched.

They are also fearful of being judged by others. They try to be extremely careful and go out of their way to not do things that could cause them embarrassment.

For a while, they are extremely fearful prior to a situation that they feel can become a disaster. It can become so bad that they lose focus and can't think straight. With social anxiety disorder, they can allow this fear to cause them to lose focus.

It doesn't matter whether it happens at school, work or at home. Having social anxiety disorder can make it difficult for the person affected to cultivate relationships with others.

With social anxiety disorder, it may be somewhat difficult for people to get over their excessive fears and concerns. This is true even if they know that what they feel is not realistic. Some will try to make amends.

Even then there is a feeling of anxiety and they don't feel comfortable when they are around other people. Then they are overly concerned of how others thought of them after the encounter.

A person could be in a social setting (for example, at dinner with someone or more than one person) and they will experience anxiety because they are fearful. They will sweat a lot, blush, shake, or find it difficult to hold a conversation with other people at the table. They always seem to feel that other people are watching them.

There are over 15 million adults in the United States alone that suffer from social anxiety disorder or social phobia. For the most part, this condition begins as a child and can continue through adolescence.

There are some studies that say genetics plays a part in this. This condition is often coupled with depression or other anxiety disorders or attacks. It is not a good idea for those affected to treat themselves with medication. It could make the situation worse. This is better treated with professionals that are experienced in this field.

- **Obsessive Compulsive Disorder**

People that deal with obsessive-compulsive disorder, or OCD, constantly have thoughts that can make them upset. In order to get their anxiety under control, they use compulsions (rituals). However, the tables end up turning on them because the rituals take control over their mind.

For instance, there are some people that are obsessed with being clean. They are known as "clean freaks". Of course, it's a good practice to want everything to stay clean, but they can get to the point of being overly controlling about germs or dirty surfaces.

They have a compulsion to wash their hands continuously. They don't want any germs or dirt to touch their hands. When they go to the bathroom, they will take a paper towel to open and close the door, just to keep from getting germs on their hands.

If people that have OCD don't feel like they look their best, they will look in the mirror several times until they feel they are presentable. They don't want to feel as though they look out of place among others.

These actions provide them with a temporary release of the anxiety that they have been feeling. People with this disorder are always compelled to check things repeatedly, or make sure that things are in the same place repeatedly.

Sometimes, they are obsessed with ideas of violence or harm to others. They also have thoughts of crazy things that people would not normally think about. There are times when they feel they have to hoard and keep things that they don't need.

There are some that have rituals in their home. One of the more common ones is checking the stove several times before they leave to make sure it is off. Having obsessive-compulsive disorder can turn into havoc and an unwelcome interruption when it happens on a daily basis.

When a person is engrained with obsessive-compulsive disorder, they know what they are doing doesn't make much sense, but they don't look at their behavior as something that is abnormal.

There are over two million adults in the United States that have obsessive-compulsive disorder. This condition does not stand out on its own. It can be combined with things such as anxiety disorders or attacks, depression or eating disorders.

This disorder affects women and men almost equally. It usually starts as a child or it can start in the teen years or even as an adults. Through research, there is an indication that OCD can happen through genetics. At least of third of all adults in the United States start out with OCD as a child.

The symptoms of obsessive-compulsive disorder can come and go at any time. If it really gets bad, it can severely affect a person from acting in a normal capacity and doing certain tasks. It's a good idea for those that are dealing with this not to use alcohol or drugs to calm them down. It just makes the situation worse for them.

There are certain treatments and medications that can be used to ward off obsessive-compulsive disorder. They can help people that are in fear or anxiety to be desensitized to what is going on around them.

- **Post-Traumatic Stress Disorder**

Post-Traumatic Stress Disorder or PTSD happens when someone has suffered something that included harm of the body or implied the threat of harm. The person who gets PTSD may have been harmed, or it may have been someone close to them.

PTSD is commonly known in regard to veterans who served in a war. However, there are other things, such as a rape, kidnapping, abuse, vehicular accidents, plane crashes or natural disasters such as hurricanes or floods.

Keep Calm and Plan

Those that suffer from Post-Traumatic Stress Disorder can be easily startled. They also have no feeling for those who they used to have a close relationship with. They start to have less interest in things they used to do. They show less affection, are increasingly aggressive and show more of the irritable side.

They try to block out things that remind them of that traumatic event instead of working through it. If the event was something that someone else deliberately acted on against them, then PTSD will greatly affect them.

Nightmares can haunt them and they start to see flashbacks such as sounds, feelings and images of what happened. There are sounds that can remind them of that event. For instance, if a door slams, then that could mean that someone has you trapped in a room and ready to pounce on you with their abuse.

It could by physical or verbal. Some people don't realize that verbal abuse is just as bad, if not worse than physical abuse.

Keep in mind that everyone who has been traumatized will not experience PTSD. Some people are able to cope with what happened and move on. There are others that need therapy and medication to deal with their issues.

PTSD can start a few months after the event or incident. It could last for a few more months, or continue through the years. In order to be officially classified as PTSD, the symptoms have to continue for at least a month. There are some who end up having PTSD as a chronic condition.

There are over seven million adults in the United States that are dealing with Post-Traumatic Stress Disorder. It can start from the childhood years and work its way up to adulthood. There are more women that suffer from this than men. PTSD is also combined with substance abuse, depression or other anxiety disorders or attacks.

CHAPTER 2- UNDERSTANDING PANIC AND PANIC ATTACKS

Panic disorder is considered to be an illness. Symptoms include feeling suddenly terrorized, feeling faint, and pain in the chest or feeling smothered. Panic attacks fall under the panic disorder condition and are prone to some of these same symptoms, plus others. When someone is having a panic attack, there are thoughts that are unrealistic or they fear that they are no longer in control or a situation.

With panic disorder, a person can also experience depression, or substance abuse. If these conditions are attached to their panic disorder, they should not be treated together. Sometimes they will feel sad or won't want to eat. They may not be able to sleep or only sleep for a few hours. They don't have much energy to do anything and they cannot maintain focus.

Steven Carter
Do You Experience Panic Attacks?

A panic attack is when a person has a fear or apprehension that is sudden or intense. There is usually nothing wrong and no one is in danger. Panic attacks can happen suddenly, last for a few minutes, and then it's over. There are others that last longer than a few minutes or there may be more than one and they follow behind one another.

There are three types of panic attacks:

Spontaneous -these panic attacks occur with no warning. There is nothing that could possibly bring it on. Even if a person is sleeping, they can still experience a panic attack.

Situationally bound - these panic attacks happen when there is a situation to which a person has been or will be exposed to. They are said to trigger or provoke the panic attack. For instance, if a person hears a car backfire, it could remind them of when they were in the military and fighting a war with ammunition.

Situationally predisposed - these panic attacks can happen when there is a delayed reaction. The attack doesn't always occur right away. There are some instances where people may immediately have an attack, and other instances it is delayed or it may not happen at all.

Panic attacks are defined as having at least four or more symptoms:

- A choking feeling
- Lightheaded or dizzy
- Shaking
- Trembling

Keep Calm and Plan

- Shortness of breath
- Accelerated heartbeat
- Pain in chest
- Numbness
- Chills
- Feeling of going crazy
- Nauseated
- Sweating
- Feelings of detachment

If a person experiences less than four symptoms, they can still be classified as having a panic attack, but it would be called a "limited symptom" panic attack. A person can have a panic attack at any time. It can even happen when they are sleeping. It has affected millions of adults in the United States.

However, there are more women that experience panic attacks. In fact, women experience panic attacks twice as much as men do. Panic attacks can start in the late teen or early adult years.

There are people that have frequent panic attacks and allow themselves to become almost helpless. There are some places where they will have stay away from because it can trigger another attack.

Or a person may not be able to participate in some activities, like going shopping and related outings. Most of the time, they are confined to where they live and won't go out unless someone else is with them.

This condition is called agoraphobia, which is when a person is fearful of open spaces or being out and about by themselves. If they seek help early for this, the progressive treatment can be successful.

It is a very treatable anxiety disorder and will respond to most medications or therapies that are provided to them. Medication and/or therapy can help the affected person to alter the way that they think in order to rid themselves of fear and anxiety.

If you have frequent panic attacks, you may have a panic disorder. Panic attacks become a panic disorder when the condition becomes chronic. Your life can be in serious danger, along with others.

CHAPTER 3- THE TELL-TALE SIGNS OF PANIC ATTACKS

If you've ever wondered the power of our minds over our bodies, then a panic attack is an excellent illustration of how powerful our thinking is over the mechanics of our bodies.

There are a range of physical symptoms our mind can generate around our bodies. As everyone is different, you may not experience all of these to experience a full panic attack. However if you experience several of these together, it is likely you are having a panic attack

- A feeling of lightheadedness or dizziness. This is often at the beginning of the attack. You can feel a little like you've had a few glasses too much to drink, or a sense the room is shifting a little around you. There may be a rushing sound in your ears, as the blood moves away from your brain, causing you to feel like you may faint.

- Difficulty in breathing. Your throat feels as if it has a large lump in it, and it hurts to swallow. Your chest tightens and constricts and it's difficult to take deep slow breaths. If feels a little like you've just been sprinting for a few kilometers and you need to catch your breath.

- Your heart rate increases. Your pulse becomes faster and fluttery and sometimes a little uneven. Your heart is thumping against your chest and you are unable to slow it even if you are sitting still.

- Hot flushes. Your face feels flushed and it feels almost as if you have a high temperature. You can also feel nauseous, as if you are trying to fight off an infection

- Waves of anxiety. The anxious feelings rise and fall through the attack as you struggle to regain control. As each wave comes it becomes a little more intense.

- Unable to stop unwanted thinking or the inability to keep control of your thinking, struggling to manage where your thoughts go. Your thoughts may skip from normal every day concern to imagined fears, fantasizing the very worst outcome of whatever you are battling. It can run as a loop inside your mind, repeating the very thoughts you lease enjoy.

- Feeling disconnected from reality. You're unable to place the way you feel with what is actually happen. Often part of you can know what you are thinking isn't correct, and it's too much, but you still can't stop. It's like there is two of you inside your mind, one stable and sensible and the other losing it- and the sensible one can't shout the panicking side down.

- Feeling out of control. Panic attacks are in the main a loss of control. From your physical manifestation of panic to your thoughts, you lose the ability to manage the way you think and act. The problem is that much of the effect is internal so while you may be deathly panicked inside, with your heart racing and your mind going all over the place, your physical body can remain completely still. It's like panic is running a marathon inside your body, and you can't work out how it can escape.

Many people confuse the sense of panic with having a heart attack. The sensation can feel almost the same. Due to this it is a very good idea to seek out professional attention to ensure there is not a physical reason for your attack.

CHAPTER 4- WHAT CAUSES PANIC ATTACKS?

Researchers are still unsure what causes panic attacks. However if other family members have suffered from them, there is a stronger likelihood that you too may do so. Stress of course can also play a large factor with panic attacks often first appearing at times of great change such as getting married, having a child, moving homes, financial stress or changing career. Sudden changes that are out of your control such as the death of someone close to you, a marriage breakup or redundancy can also trigger a panic attack, particularly if there were additional stressors ongoing at the same time.

If you have a close relative who is bipolar or suffers from depression, then your chances of suffering from a panic attack greatly increase.

However there are several physical ailments and conditions that can also share the same physical feelings as a panic attack. It is a very good idea to check these things are not causing your panicked feelings.

Mitral valve prolapse. This is when one of the heart valves does not close off properly. It is not a major condition but should be diagnosed and treated to prevent further complications.

Tachycardia. You may experience a raised heart rate due to a tachycardia attack. This may be a symptom of another heart related syndrome and your doctor will probably suggest an ECG to check for any illegalities.

Hyperthyroidism. This is also often accompanied with a loss of appetite and weight loss. This can be checked with a simple blood test and is treatable. Hyperthyroidism is caused by an over active thyroid.

Hypoglycemia. A very low blood sugar count can send your body into overdrive as it tries to protect the brain and keeps it functioning. This can also be a precursor to diabetes. A test of your glucose tolerance can help earmark whether this could be an issue for you.

Overuse of stimulants. Anything that artificially increases the heart rate such as too many coffees and energy drinks, illegal drugs such as cocaine, or the use of amphetamines can cause you to display some of the same characteristics.

Adjusting to a change of medication. If you've been on a course of medication for a length of time and then taken yourself off it, sometimes there can be a physical reaction as your brain adjusts to the different chemicals in your body. If you are on a medication long term, consult your doctor before coming off it as they may have some suggestions on how to provide your body with the best way to have little to no reaction to the change.

Running on empty. If you live in a constant state of flux, with high stress levels you may be suffering from adrenal failure which can trigger panic attacks. Adrenal failure is a growing problem in today's busy life and can lead to hyperthyroidism and other complications if not treated.

Depression can bring on panic attacks. It's important to look at the whole range of feelings and symptoms you are dealing with.

While it is possible to alter your behavior, and learn simple methods to cope, it is equally as important to ensure you receive the correct medication to help you while you learn these methods if necessary.

Besides the situations reasons mentioned above, researchers are unsure about the exact reason for panic attacks. In many ways it's just our bodies designed to do what they should, but in our modern world our bodies do not have the same required need to run out or stress, being chased by a saber toothed tiger who wants his dinner.

Our natural defense system against stress is our flight and fight response which is one of our most basic and primitive action and also one of our most powerful. It's meant to be powerful as it's meant to protect us from moving buses, falling trees and anything else that may come between us and life. This flight of fight response speeds up your heart, pumping adrenaline into your blood to get you ready to run for your life. Our poor bodies have not evolved as fast as our world, so while our brain is telling us to run, our bodies stall nice and still, or sitting quietly somewhere.

The fight or flight response is meant to help you either stand and cope with the danger, or run away from it. It's normal and it's natural. What makes a panic attack difference is there is no danger- it's just the expectation or preemptive possibility of danger that's triggering it.

While some panic attacks can be attributed to a family history of panic attacks, or to a psychological disorder, they can also occur with no clear reason.

CHAPTER 5- STRESS AND PANIC ATTACKS

People who live stressful, high powered lives are more likely than others to suffer from panic attacks. As the stress in our lives becomes more intense the pressure increases. It's a little like one of those whistling kettles that explode with steam and noise once they get to the right temperature. The pressure builds and builds until there is nowhere for it to go but course through your body. The more stress you place on your body and mind every day, the closer you are at all times to that boiling point.

Our brain is very clever. It is constantly checking and rechecking to make sure we have all the reactions and chemicals we need to live our lives. It is always ready to kick start our flight or fight response, ready to protect us against whatever s our enemy. It can't tell the difference between a real saber toothed tiger and a metaphorical one, but to all intents and purposes, the tiger is just as dangerous and we need protecting from it. The panic attack is merely our body trying to look after us the way our bodies have been caring for us since we first experienced stress.

Just because our brain thinks its life threatening doesn't mean that it is. It just means our most primitive part of our body, the part that works completely on instinct rather than logic or reason has decided we need a bit of a kick start. This can be either because we're living on a constant rollercoaster of stress or because something in our environment has reminded us of something we associate with danger and the need for a flight or fight reaction.

If you've ever brushed past a car alarm, barely touching it and it's gone off you'll know how easy it can be to set off something incredibly sensitive. Our flight or fight response can be like that too. We can become so sensitive that it starts up at the smallest incident and it's difficult to stop it once its screams of protest against danger have begun.

The solution is simple. If we go back to our whistling kettle, the simplest way to stop it boiling, letting all that steam and noise go is to turn down the heat. Our panic attacks can be managed or prevented in the same way. All we need to do is turn down the heat. Even if the day to day stress remains, we can learn to manage it at a simmering boil, rather than at a fast and furious froth of bubbles and heat.

Chapter 6- Delaying Treatments Could Lead to More Serious Effects

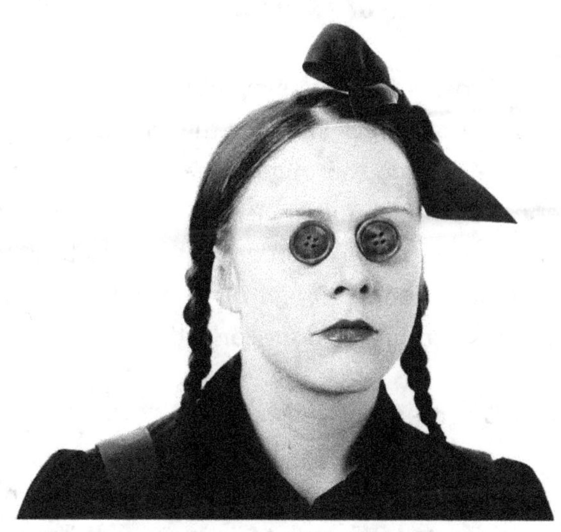

If you are experiencing some kind of panic attacks then, you must start a solution as soon as possible because if you delay the cure then, situation will become more and more dangerous and worse with every passing day. Everything starts from physical checkup and tests and when everything seems fine then, you need to consult some good psychologist to help you in this case.

He will know the symptoms and feelings which you can go through while experiencing panic attacks. Proper and healthy diet introduction can lead to less panic attacks and sleep is another very effective tool to help you in panic situations. People often suffer from sleeping disorder as a first symptom of panic attacks and if you are also going through this disorder then make it to go away as soon as possible.

There are so many other techniques available to control panic attacks and these techniques include distraction techniques, deep breathing techniques, muscle relaxation exercises and lot others and all of these techniques can help to reduce the frequency of these panic attacks and if you act on them regularly then you can even get rid of panic attacks completely.

The Importance of Proper Medication

Panic disorder is more relevant to mental disorder and there is very less medication available for this problem but doctors have done a very intense and thorough research on this subject and found some very effective medications. These medications may not be a full cure for your panic disorder but they do treat you up to 70 percent and rest is done through other treatment methods like different kinds of therapies and similar activities.

Panic Disorder Has No Medicine

Normally it is said that panic attacks cannot be treated with medicines and it is true to some extant because the core disorder of panic cannot be cured with medicines but its symptoms can be controlled with this medication easily. These symptoms and you can also call them effects of panic disorder like fast breathing, sweating, headache and other similar problems can be well-controlled with medicines. Normally doctors prescribe anti-depressant medicines to panic disorder patients because these medicines are made to relieve the mind and they give a sense of extra relaxation to patient's mind. He forgets about the tension and that situation in which he or she goes in panic state.

You can say that panic attacks are acute anxiety and when anxiety reaches to its worst state then, it becomes panic and it remains in that way unless or until you find a solution to this problem. You should never ignore the signs of panic attacks and do something about them as soon as possible.

Panic Disorder Is Not a Physical Illness

You need to know that panic disorder is not a physical illness instead it is just a mental response to certain tense and awkward situations. When your mind faces some uncertain and unbelievable event then, he responds in a very reluctant way and this reluctant way sometimes causes some confusion.

This is the reason that most of the therapists and physicians believe that this kind of mental illness cannot be completely cured with medication and in fact there is no proper medication available for this purpose. All the medicines which are prescribed are for temporary control and for mental relief. Therapies like cognitive behavior therapy and relaxation therapies are more widely used for treatment of panic disorder.

Medicines Commonly Prescribed

Medication is not the cure all for anxiety disorders, attacks and related conditions. However, medication can control these conditions while the person is receiving therapy. Medication can only be used if a physician prescribes it.

They are usually prescribed by psychiatrists that offer therapy of work with colleagues that provide some of the same services. For the most part, the medications that are used for anxiety disorders are:

• Antidepressants

• Anti-anxiety drugs

• Beta-blockers

Using any of these medications can help the person to live a normal life.

Antidepressants

Originally, antidepressants were used for treatment of depression. However, they also work for those that are suffering from anxiety disorders. They work to change the chemistry in the brain. Once the initial dose is taken, it takes at least 4 to 6 weeks before the symptoms will go away. The medication must be taken as directed in order for this to work.

- **SSRIs (Selective Serotonin Reuptake Inhibitors)**

These antidepressants work to change the level of the communication of the brain cells. Some of the more common ones are Prozac, Zoloft and Lexapro.

They are used to treat any panic disorder that is mixed with social phobia, depression or OCD. Since these are newer, they don't have as many side effects. However, those that use them may experience being jittery or nauseated in the initial stages of taking them. This is only temporary.

- **Tricyclics**

These antidepressants are older than SSRIs and are used for anxiety disorders other than OCD. They are administered with a low dosage and increase gradually.

Side effects include being dizzy, dry mouth, drowsy and weight gain. This can be eliminated by adjusting the dosage or using another medication of the same kind of antidepressant. Tofranil is used for GAD and panic disorder; Anafranil is used for OCD.

• MAOIs (Monoamine Oxidase Inhibitors)

These are the oldest of the antidepressants available to use for these conditions. It is mostly used for anxiety disorders, attacks and related conditions.

Some of the more common ones are Nardil, Marplan and Parnate. When taking MAOIs, there are certain foods and drinks that you have to stay away from. That would include cheese and red wine.

In addition to that, you cannot take Advil, Motrin, Tylenol or any other pain, cold or allergy reliever medication. Plus, women will not be able to use certain types of birth control pills. Herbal supplements are also off limits. Mixing MAOIs with any of these can cause an adverse reaction.

• Anti-Anxiety Drugs

Drugs such as benzodiazepines are highly potent. They work to fight off anxiety and have very few side effects. Being drowsy is the only one that is noticeable. This drug is only prescribed for a brief period of time. Physicians are weary about providing them to past drug abusers.

Because people can get easily addicted to them, they look for additional doses so they can keep going. However, if the person has panic disorder, they can use these drugs up to a year.

For social phobia, Klonpin is used and Ativan is used for panic disorder. One of the most common antidepressants on the market is Xanax, which is used for GAD and panic disorder.

If a person stops taking benzodiazepines all of a sudden, they can experience withdrawals; the anxiety attacks can come back to haunt them. This is one reason why some physicians are leery about using this drug or use them sporadically.

Another anti-anxiety medication is Busiprone and it is used for GAD. There are some side effects that include nausea, headaches or dizziness. This is taken different than benzodiazepines. Busiprone has to be taken every day for at least two week before a person will feel the anti-anxiety effect from the drug.

- **Beta-Blockers**

Beta-blockers are used for treatment of heart conditions. They can also be used to keep away physical symptoms that determine anxiety disorders. Beta-blockers are used in situations such as if a person is giving a speech in front of other people, a bet-blocker can be used to keep those symptoms at bay.

If you are taking medication for an anxiety disorder, you should do the following:

- Have your physician to advise you on what medication would be effective for your condition.

- Have the physician consult you on how the drug works and what are the side effects from taking the drug.

- Inform your physician of other medications you may be taking. They may interfere with the dosage of the drug anxiety disorders.

The physician should advise you on the dosage and how you are directed to take it. They also need to advise you on how you should stop taking it when the time comes. With medication, some of them can actually trigger systems that can cause panic attacks.

Steven Carter
Physicians should always start out with a lower dose and then work their way up.

CHAPTER 7- IS COGNITIVE THERAPY EFFECTIVE FOR PANIC PATIENTS?

Cognitive behavior therapy is a types of psychotherapy which emphasis on the role of thinking and its impacts. It tries to get thoughts clean and helps the patients to overcome their negative thoughts. Cognitive behavior therapy is a more general term which includes some other therapies in it too and it consists of parts.

There are different techniques as Rational Emotive Behavior Therapy, Rational Behavior Therapy, Rational Living Therapy, Cognitive Therapy, and Dialectic Behavior Therapy. All of these therapies are included in the general type of cognitive behavior therapy.

Cognitive Behavior Therapy Depends Upon Emotional Response

In this therapy, it is not considered that our actions occur due to our surrounding physical factors instead in cognitive behavior therapy it is believed that our actions are caused due to our thoughts and our thoughts can impact on our overall behavior. The beauty of this therapy is that by changing our thoughts, we can change our surroundings and actions.

Cognitive behavior therapy is not only effective against panic disorder but it is also used in many mental diseases and its results are very satisfactory. Long researches have been carried out about this subject and lots of literature is published about this subject but people are still unaware about the full effectiveness of this therapy. Over last few years the popularity of cognitive behavior therapy has gained popularity and there are different reasons for this popularity.

First of all, in past few decades, there has been a gradual increase in mental and psychological problems, and CBT has proved a very decent way and effective against these mental and psychological disorders. There is a very structured, planned and in most of the cases very effective approach towards these problems. Another very important thing which is increasing the popularity of CBT is no medication involved and people prefer those methods of treatment which do not involve heavy medication.

What is CBT?

Cognitive behavior therapy is a type of psychological treatment which works by finding the correlation between our thoughts, feelings and actions. There is a time limited for this whole therapy to complete and normally this time period is less than a 2-3 months and it includes 10-15 sessions.

CBT is also known as family of mental treatments because different approaches are mixed and are implemented in a more collective and effective manner. CBT is known to be effective for people who have been undergoing other treatment as well or they have tried other treatments and have failed to cure.

You can also say that CBT is a process in which people are trained to think positive and their negative thoughts are eliminated. Thinking has a very deep effect on our daily life and multiple people seeing same event can interpret that event in different ways. For example if a glass of water is half filled then, some people will say that glass is half empty which is a discouraging thought while others can say glass is half filled which changes the whole approach.

Similarly, a person who is suffering from a panic attack may remember the gestures of a person who discouraged him but he will never remember the gestures of a person who appreciates him. These negative thinking adds more pressure and makes the situation tenser and sever.

CBT is the process to control these negative thoughts and bring the positive thoughts in front. In short, you can say that CBT tells you to control your thought which allows your mind to think more positively and more energetically. All of these things, if properly implemented, Can result in temporary or sometime permanent relief to panic disorder.

Improving Behaviors

Our thoughts affect our behavior and things which we think, we often execute and those things become our behavior and this behavior is needed to be changed which is done in CBT. A person who is going through a panic disorder is often facing lot more increases tension than a person who has forethought about that situation and adjusted according to the condition. This is the key thing which is to make adjustment according to your surroundings.

Parts of Therapy

The core therapy consists of different parts which are needed to be executed very precisely and accurately.

Relationship between Patient and Therapist

In order to make CBT more effective, practitioner of CBT which is an expert in his filed and patient, who is expert of his life, should cooperate and understand each other thoroughly. When a friendly environment is created and patient starts to share everything then, the problems begin to vanish and results start to come.

Goal Setting

Once the problem has been identified then, it is necessary for the practitioner to set a goal that how many sessions or how much time will be consumed to get that person again on track. This is important because as I mentioned above that CBT is always a limited time treatment.

Start Focusing on Present

This is obvious that you can never change your past but by thinking less about past, we can definitely make our present little better. Encouraging thought can make your future better because when you think less about your distressed past then, you feel new hope and strength to move ahead but if you keep thinking about the negatives of past then, it will become really hard for you to move on. It does not mean that you should totally forget your past instead you just need to remember past as a learning lesson and do not over pose your past in your present.

For example, if a person had a panic attack while addressing in public then, he will definitely feel very distress while going and addressing in public again but you need to make sure that you do not allow that past fear to overcome your mind. Start thinking it as a new day and try new things.

A CBT therapist will do the same and he will talk into the fears of patient and will change the perception of the patient about that particular event. Person experiences different beliefs and his whole perception of panicking from that situation changes.

CBT is Structured

As I mentioned above that time for CBT is predetermined and normally it is determined after first session. One session is not more than one hour in length. A qualified practitioner always sets up an agenda before every session which decides that which topics he is going to cover in a particular session and this agenda depends upon the problem of patient.

In fact, the between-session practice is also preplanned and patient is made to believe in treatment and he is encouraged and made ready to be cured. This kind of structured approach is beneficial and it produces very defined, concrete and fast results.

The Formulation of Treatment

By gathering all the data about patients, CBT practitioner makes a very fixed plan of treatment and this plan is normally made after a long research which includes the logs from hundreds of patients and their behavioral and physical gestures.

This is also an effective technique because lots of people can have similar problem and if you start keeping track of patients then, you can find an easy solution to certain common problems.

For example, if a person is going through panic attacks then, it is for sure that he has some trigger point which makes him afraid and he goes through panic. In order to make him normal, you need to make sure that he becomes so strong mentally that he faces his fear and once he faced his fear and realized that it was just a thought in his mind then, he will start taking that triggering point normal.

Chapter 8- If Medication and Therapy Are Not Enough

Other than taking medication and therapy, there are alternative treatments that can be used in order to combat these conditions in the anxiety and panic attack family.

One of the main keys to getting over anxiety and panic attacks is to relax. That's not as easy to do as some may think. Start out by focusing and making sure that you are breathing slowly and steadily.

When a person is having a panic attack, one of the first things that happens is they have trouble breathing. Sometimes they have to pant in order to catch their breath. The purpose here is to make your breaths even so that they will slow down your heart rate.

This will help the panic attack to eventually go away. A person is able to calm themselves by breathing slowly. They must continue to release air from their lungs. This helps to have deep breaths and make them feel calmer.

Lying down with your backside near a wall, bend the knees with the feet against the wall. Use one foot at a time and press into the wall. As you press it in, breathe in. As you release it from the wall, breathe out. Change up your feet when you are doing this. Take about 15 minutes until the feeling of panic has lifted from you.

Try not to think about the past. A lot of times, panic attacks happen from something that has to do with your past that you were upset about. Look at different shapes and colors. If you like pets, get a small dog or cat and love on it.

If you are into fragrances, you can use aromatherapy to relieve yourself of anxiety and panic attacks. One aroma that has a calming effect is lavender. There are many places where you can purchase essential oils.

When you feel an anxiety or panic attack coming on, sniff the oil and it will work to calm you down. You can also use it as massage oil, along with olive or grape seed oil. There are other aromatherapy oils you can use. You have to smell them to see which one you prefer.

Relaxation Techniques

Relaxation techniques are a known method to treat panic disorder and these techniques are being used throughout the world. People have different opinions about these techniques but now days, as depression and mental disorders have increased, people have started to trust these techniques as an effective method to heal and help people in their mental disorders. In this discussion, I will discuss some of the known relaxation techniques which can help you in controlling your panic attacks.

Quick Relaxation

There are some exercises which can work wonders for you. For example if you just get some lose cloths and get comfortable, it sends a very soothing signal to mind. Get your toe muscles tight and hold them in tight position for 10 seconds then, release them and you will experience a great sense of relaxation in your whole body.

You can do this with all the other muscles of your body too because getting muscles in tension and then releasing that tension feels very relaxing and soothing for your whole body. Deep and slow breathing during this muscle relaxation is also helpful.

Process of Long Term Relaxation

The above mentioned exercises are just for short term relief and relaxation but when it comes to relaxing your mind then, you always need some strong relaxation techniques. People use relaxation techniques to get out of panic situation but those relaxation techniques need lots of practice to be learned properly. Now I will tell you some of those techniques in this discussion.

Meditate Your Thoughts

When people hear the word meditation then, they normally think that it will include some long and tiring exercise in which they have to sit and practice some unique exercise. This is not the proper mediation instead according to a certified physician the definition of meditation is stated as

"Any repetitive action can be source of meditation"

From this definition, it is evident that all the techniques like swimming, painting knitting and others can be a source of meditation for a particular person. In more brief way, you can say that any action which can keep your mind and thoughts in present is taken as meditation.

Your Surrounding Environment Matters

The environment in which you live has a very important role to play in making your thoughts positive and negative. Consciously, you cannot realize the difference between environments but you must have observed that it is easier to relax in certain parts of the house for example you may feel more relaxed in TV lounge than in your bedroom.

This can happen and you need to find that perfect corner of your house to relax where your body and mind can synchronize effectively. If you feel comfortable in certain set of accessories then, you should equip your bed room with those and make sure that when you relax then, it is 100 percent relaxing and your mind is not distracted anywhere.

Productivity Not Procrastination

This is another important thing to know that relaxation does not mean that you should become unproductive and spend your whole day sitting on your sofa and watching TV because this will make you dizzier and your mind will start to go into a different state.

Relaxation is about finding time to relax your mind during the usual activities throughout the day. Relaxing allows you to work with greater concentration and keeps your mind fresh.

Chapter 9- Of Myths and Skipped Treatments

Attacks can feel like a very private terror. On the outside you can look like everything is perfectly fine, while your insides feel like they are going to explode. Many people suffering from panic attacks can feel they are isolated and set apart from others for having the attacks. However the problem is reasonably common and widespread. Many people have suffered from them, and large numbers of those have found methods to reduce or remove panic attacks entirely.

There are some common beliefs about panic attacks that sufferers hold. Perhaps you have experienced some of these yourself.

1. It's going to make your heart give out, and you'll die. Regardless of how hard your heart is pounding in your chest, it's far stronger than you give it credit for. It's the strongest muscle in our bodies and it's designed to be able to take a rapid increase- just as it would if you were running a marathon or doing a funky dance class. If you do have an existing heart condition it is perhaps best to get it checked just for peace of mind, but for the vast majority our hearts will be completely fine during and after an attack.

2. You won't get enough air to your lungs. Many people find it hard to breathe well during a panic attack. However you are actually taking in more air than you feel like you are. The tightness and then accompanying lightness of breath is caused by hyperventilation, with your breaths causing an excess of oxygen to move through your body.

3. You may faint. You won't faint because your body is trying to protect you from danger. If it was a physical threat your body would want to keep you upright and moving very fast away from danger. Even if your danger isn't a physical one, your body is actually increasing your consciousness and you are incredibly awake. If worst comes to worst and you did faint, think of the benefits. At least you'd have some rest from the thumping in your chest if you did faint. The sense that you might faint comes from the hyperventilation. Even though you feel weak and as if you may faint, your large muscles are soaking in oxygen and are pumped and ready for action.

4. You feel as is you may be having a stroke. Because your body is feeling a wide range of sensations you may try to work out what is causing it. However all the physical sensations are not from a deeper issue such as a stroke. Your body isn't about to self-destruct. It's just doing a very natural thing in a time of extreme stress.

5. You are going crazy. Because you don't feel like you are in control the whole experience can felt like you are unbalanced or losing your mind. However all that is happening is your body is reacting to the need to escape whatever situation you've found yourself in. That is a very sane solution to your needs.

6. You are worried you are going to embarrass yourself. Panic attacks are very personal things. What sets one person off is different to what would set off another person. Remember that while you feel like everyone can see how you are feeling; most of what you are experiencing isn't noticeable to anyone else. Most panic attacks last less than ten minutes, and certainly no longer than twenty. It will pass, and once it's gone things quickly come back to normal again.

7. You're completely out of control. Actually you are still in control- just a different part of your brain is organizing your body. Your body is allowing your subconscious mind to take over so that your conscious mind stops second guessing it. Your body is still being taken care of, just by a different part of your brain.

Remembering the panic attack will pass is perhaps the first step in conquering the attacks and learning how to manage them.

What If It's Left Untreated?

Left untreated panic attacks occurring on a regular basis can develop into agoraphobia. It's one of the reasons why it's good to seek treatment as early as possible.

Agoraphobia kicks in when a person suffering for panic attacks starts to worry about having one in a public place where they are unable to hide the effects of it from others. It may be a place they cannot easily escape from, or where people may easily notice them. Approximately thirty percent of panic attack sufferers develop agoraphobia.

Are you at risk of developing agoraphobia? If you have experienced some of the following symptoms, it is advisable to go have a chat to your doctor about whether agoraphobia is a potential problem for you.

Agoraphobics are afraid of the following:

*Being in an open place. You feel exposed and vulnerable when you don't have clearly defined physical boundaries

*Entering public places, go shopping or be part of a crowd. It can almost feel the adverse of agoraphobic with a sense that everything is closing in and feeling stifling. Escape is the only thing you want.

*Traveling in planes, busses and trains where you are part of the crowd.

*Being in a lift or on a bridge. Anything that cannot be escaped from easily.

*A café, movie theatre or restaurant that you cannot walk out of whenever you want to.

*Any location that is unfamiliar and different. Many agoraphobics become virtual recluses, preferring to stay at home where everything is more easily controlled.

People who suffer from panic attacks can also develop other phobias or OCD. These fears are developed when your mind naturally wants to avoid those foods or types of exercise or behaviors that you feel may be setting your panic attacks off. This in turn creates a greater likelihood of fresh panic attacks if you are placed in front of these stimuli.

Avoiding Foods that Make You Panic

If you have sensitivity to a particular type of food, eating it can increase your likelihood of having a panic attack. There are a few types of foods that can trigger an attack but in particular there are three chief ones that can affect your ability to keep that panic in check.

The top three anxiety producing foods are sugar, alcohol and caffeine. These three don't cause the panic attack, but they can increase your general state of anxiety which can compound the problem.

Sugar

Many people today use sugar as their emergency pick me up food. This creates a huge wave of mood changes as you move from a low sugar state to a high one and then come crashing back down again. The craving for sugary foods or high carbs such as doughnuts and cakes often indicates a sugar addiction problem. Eating sugar can cause lactic acid to build up in your bloodstream. High levels of this can bring on a panicky state of mind.

Sugary food needs insulin to counteract it in the bloodstream. The body releases large amounts of insulin that reduces the amount of sugar in your blood. This can cause an agitated state of mind and your mood can swing as the sugar rises and falls. If you have a tendency to suffer from panic attacks, it is a good idea to go on a low GI or low sugar diet. As refined carbohydrates also convert to sugar fast it is best to stick to natural foods with plenty of whole grains, vegetables and good protein.

Alcohol

Alcohol is both a stimulant and an exaggerant. Whatever your state of mind, alcohol will help you get there bigger and faster. Drinking alcohol also increases the lactic acid in your body, and causes your blood sugar levels to exaggerate. It also prevents you from being able to make reasoned decisions or see things calmly and dispassionately.

Caffeine

Caffeine may make you feel like you are getting started in the morning, but it can be wreaking havoc with your with your ability to handle stress and your levels of panicky feelings. Caffeine can block the protein adenosine which regulates the firing of neurons in the brain. This protein is the one that causes you to feel drowsy. Caffeine affects its ability to kick start the process, increasing the firing of the neurons. This makes your body produce adrenaline because your body thinks an emergency is close by. The adrenaline increase can cause your heart rate to increase, and increases your body's state of emergency. This can be enough to make you feel anxious.

Caffeine also increases the lactic acid build up in your body. If you think you are drinking too much caffeine form both coffee and from carbonated caffeine drinks such as energy drinks and cola, then slowly reduce the amount you are drinking to remove the problem. Watch your caffeine intake from all sorts of sources-green tea, which has good health benefits, also has a high amount of caffeine.

Chapter 10- First Aid Tips for Panic Attacks

Getting your breathing under control is the key to gaining control during a panic attack. Over breathing, or hyperventilation makes the intensity of the panic attack worse. It is both a symptom and a cause of the panic attack so it's important to address it.

Many people who suffer from panic attacks tend to over breathe even when they are not experiencing a panic attack.

"I discovered a simple solution to my panic attacks was to focus on my breath, breathing in deeply and slowly then pushing my breath out consciously on the exhale. I would repeat a phrase over and over again to focus my breath which I made up, but discovered was also an ancient Buddhist saying that was developed for meditation.

I would think "breathe in love" on the inhale, and "breathe out fear" on the exhale. It would stop the panic attack from taking root and I learnt to use it the first hint of time I started to move into that cycle." Emma Chilster (34)

It is important to first realize that hyperventilating is just giving you too much oxygen. Because you are putting it into your body so fast, your body doesn't have enough carbon dioxide to counteract it. Because of this the body can't use all the oxygen which makes you feel short of air.

If during a panic attack you feel light headed, dizzy and giddy, short of breath and numb in your extremities with a tight chest and a thumping heart, then you are hyperventilating. You may also have clammy hands, a dry mouth and feel as if you are breaking into a sweat. You could be shivering and feel weak all over. You may want to sit down.

Breathing evenly and regularly will dissipate the problem. There are several easy methods to help you do this.

1. Find a paper bag and breathe in and out into it. This means you get a bigger dose of carbon dioxide to compensate for the excess oxygen

2. Stop breathing. Or rather hold onto the last breath you took and let the oxygen in your body move to the place it should be. If you can do this once or twice for ten to fifteen seconds it should remove the problem

3. Go for a run. Make your heart rate go up and you'll be using up all that adrenaline too. Regular exercise also helps you to reduce stress levels over all.

Keep Calm and Plan
Panic attacks are experienced by a huge range of people from all walks of life. However they don't need to be a life sentence and are treatable. Learning to manage that first onset of panic will help free you and help you get your control back.

Be a Good Support Partner

If you are helping someone who has one of these conditions, it is very important that you are there for the long haul. It may take longer than a few weeks or months for that person to totally overcome this.

You should not be judgmental or condescending in any way to the person who is suffering. This is a serious matter and you should treat it as such. The worst thing you could do regarding anxiety and panic attacks is to be dismissive and think that they can quickly get over it. You cannot be the savior for them and solve their problem.

People who suffer these kinds of attacks are not thinking about anything except how scared they are that something bad is going to happen. The situation cannot be solved by shaking them and making them come out of it, or waving a magic wand over them and saying "abracadabra".

Don't underestimate their actions by thinking that they are pretending to be acting. This is serious and their actions should not be underestimated. The best thing you can do is to do everything in your power that you can to be there as that support system.

They could feel at any moment that they were in grave danger. They feel as though they could not pull themselves out of whatever trouble they perceived. This is when the accelerated heartbeat, shortness of breath and other symptoms come in to play.

If you ignore them, you are doing more to hurt them than to help. They depend on your support and if you decide to bail out on their weakest moment, they will feel more worthless.

This could make them start feeling depressed and not want to do much of anything for their situation. If they know that you are with them to help them stick it out, then they will feel better about themselves.

You must allow them to go through the attack. If you try to intervene, you could make the situation worse. Let it happen and they will eventually come out of it. However, if for some reason they don't stop, call a paramedic to assist.

One thing that you don't want to do is to give them medication, especially if it's not prescribed by their physician. That will definitely cause them harm. So make sure that you are not doing anything to jeopardize their well-being.

There is hope for those who have been suffering for a long time with anxiety disorders, attacks, and panic attacks. You have to be willing to make the move to make changes in your life. There are other people out there that are suffering just like you.

However, your situation doesn't have to stay this way forever. There is help out there in the form of medication, and therapy. You just have to want it for yourself. The sooner you get the help, the better you will get. Once you do that, you will stop allowing these conditions to control your life.

ABOUT THE AUTHOR

Steven Carter was born to a poor family in Australia. At the age of 13 years old, he was adopted by an American couple and was brought to the US.

His first few years in the foreign country were not at all difficult because Steven was curious and very outspoken. When he reached high school, he was elected as the class president. In college, he was the recipient of full scholarship.

Today, Steven attends to patients in the psychiatric ward.